TIME FOR KIDS

UNSOLVED!

Mysterious Events

Lisa Greathouse
Stephanie Kuligowski

I0808064

Consultants

Timothy Rasinski, Ph.D.
Kent State University

Lori Oczkus
Literacy Consultant

Based on writing from *TIME For Kids. TIME For Kids* and the *TIME For Kids* logo are registered trademarks of TIME Inc. Used under license.

Publishing Credits

Dona Herweck Rice, *Editor-in-Chief*
Lee Aucoin, *Creative Director*
Jamey Acosta, *Senior Editor*
Heidi Fiedler, *Editor*
Lexa Hoang, *Designer*
Stephanie Reid, *Photo Editor*
Rane Anderson, *Contributing Author*
Rachelle Cracchiolo, *M.S.Ed., Publisher*

Image Credits: p.11 Alamy; pp.16–17, 18 (bottom) David Parker/Photo Researchers, Inc.; p.18 (top), pp.28–29, 39 (top left) iStockphoto; pp.34–35 NASA; pp.6–7, 14 (left) EPA/Newscom; pp.15, 19 (middle) Solent News/Splash News/ Newscom; pp.4, 36–37 WENN/Newscom; pp.19 (top), 32 ZUMA Press/Newscom; All other images from Shutterstock.

Teacher Created Materials
5301 Oceanus Drive
Huntington Beach, CA 92649-1030
http://www.tcmpub.com

ISBN 978-1-4333-4827-3
© 2013 Teacher Created Materials, Inc.
Printed by: 51497
Printed in: China

Table of Contents

A Mysterious World

There have been many advances in science and technology. But many things about our world remain mysterious. In Thailand, glowing balls of light rise up from a river once a year. In Honduras, fish rain down from the sky every summer. In the California desert, huge rocks slide across the ground when no one is watching.

These strange **phenomena** (fi-NOM-uh-nuh) may seem like science fiction. But the events in this book are scientific fact. They have been seen by many people. They have been photographed and studied by scientists. And yet they remain unsolved mysteries.

In Honduras, fish rain from the sky every year.

In Thailand, glowing balls of light rise up from a river once a year.

THINK LINK

Truth can be stranger than fiction. Scientists study our world and try to explain why things happen. But scientists can't explain these freaky phenomena.

- Why do you think people see creatures that don't exist?
- How can we explain events when no one can see or witness them?
- Why is it important to investigate these strange events?

Spooky Sights and Sounds

The world is full of strange sights and sounds. There are glowing **orbs** and balls of lightning that hover in the air. There are intense booms. And there are rocks that ring like bells. Millions of people have been lucky enough to see and hear these mysterious phenomena!

Religious Rites

The Naga fireballs come like clockwork at the end of a **Buddhist** (BOO-dist) retreat. Some Buddhists believe that the Naga dragons in the Mekong River shoot the fireballs into the air to celebrate the **religious** holiday.

Floating Balls of Fire

For a few nights every October, people in Thailand see a strange light show. Glowing orbs rise from the Mekong River. The lights range in size from tiny sparks to spheres as big as basketballs. They glow red and pink as they float into the sky. Locals call these **Naga** fireballs. The Naga are dragons believed to live in the river. Scientists say gases from the river bottom rise to the surface and **ignite**. It happens every year. But researchers are still trying to explain this event.

Nature's Jack-o'-Lanterns

In the United States and Canada, floating lights are often seen in swamps and bogs. They are called *will-o'-the-wisps, jack-o'-lanterns, hinkypunks*, or *fairy lights*. Scientists say that decaying plants emit chemicals. This process can produce flickering lights.

Boing, Boing, Zap

For hundreds of years, ball lightning has baffled scientists. Witnesses tell of glowing balls that hover in the air. Sometimes, they bounce off the ground, sizzle, spin, or spark. They can even melt through glass and metal! The lightning balls appear suddenly indoors and fade away quickly. Sometimes they even explode.

The orbs can vary in size. Some are as small as a tennis ball. Others are as large as a beach ball. They usually occur during storms. There are nearly 10,000 accounts of ball lightning. But scientists have been unable to explain this strange phenomenon.

Eyewitness Account

In 2011, Rose Bellamy was taking cover from a massive tornado headed toward Joplin, Missouri. A strange sight caught her attention. She told a local newspaper, "I saw balls of fire in the backyard, big balls of red fire about the size of basketballs bobbing along across the backyard. I have no idea what it was."

Phenomenal Proof

In 2007, scientists tested the **theory** that lightning strikes soil and makes a **vapor**. With this experiment, they were able to create ball lightning in the lab. Their results are giving scientists a better understanding of how this mysterious phenomenon occurs in nature.

Step 1

Lightning strikes soil that's rich in elements such as **silicon**, aluminum, or iron.

Step 2

Heat from the lightning transforms the soil into a vapor.

Step 3

The vapor combines with the air and begins burning.

Step 4

The vapor floats through the air in small glowing orbs.

Step 5

Within 10 seconds, the glowing balls disappear or explode.

Rock Music

Ringing Rocks State Park in Pennsylvania is a unique place. It is an open field of boulders in the middle of the forest. That is weird. But there is something even stranger at this park. The rocks make music!

The ringing rocks are made of **diabase**. Diabase is a type of rock in Earth's crust. When struck with a hammer, the rocks ring like bells. All the rocks are made of the same thing. But it appears only some of them make music. Some people believe all the rocks in the park can ring. But some may make sounds that are too low for humans to hear. Scientists have not figured out how the ringing happens.

In 1890, Dr. J. J. Ott gave the world's first rock concert, playing the ringing rocks with a hammer.

World Music

Ringing rocks have been found in Pennsylvania, Montana, Mexico, England, Scotland, and Australia.

Visitors may be tempted to take a ringing rock home, but they will be disappointed. The rocks lose their musical sound when they are away from the other rocks.

Sound Effects

People around the world have reported hearing loud booms. The sounds were not made by storms. They were not made by humans. But they are strong enough to shake houses! Scientists have many theories about the booms. Some think they may be caused by small earthquakes. Others point to mud volcanoes. Still other people guess they may be from meteors or booming sands. But researchers have yet to find proof.

These strange sounds have been heard all over. People on the North Carolina coast and in upstate New York have heard the booms. They have also been heard in Belgium and Italy. And booms have been heard in India and Japan, too.

One Phenomenon, Many Names

People in Belgium call the big booms *mistpouffers*, which means "fog belches." In Italy they are called *brontidi*. In the 1800s, author James Fenimore Cooper coined the term *Seneca guns* for the sounds that shake Lake Seneca in upstate New York.

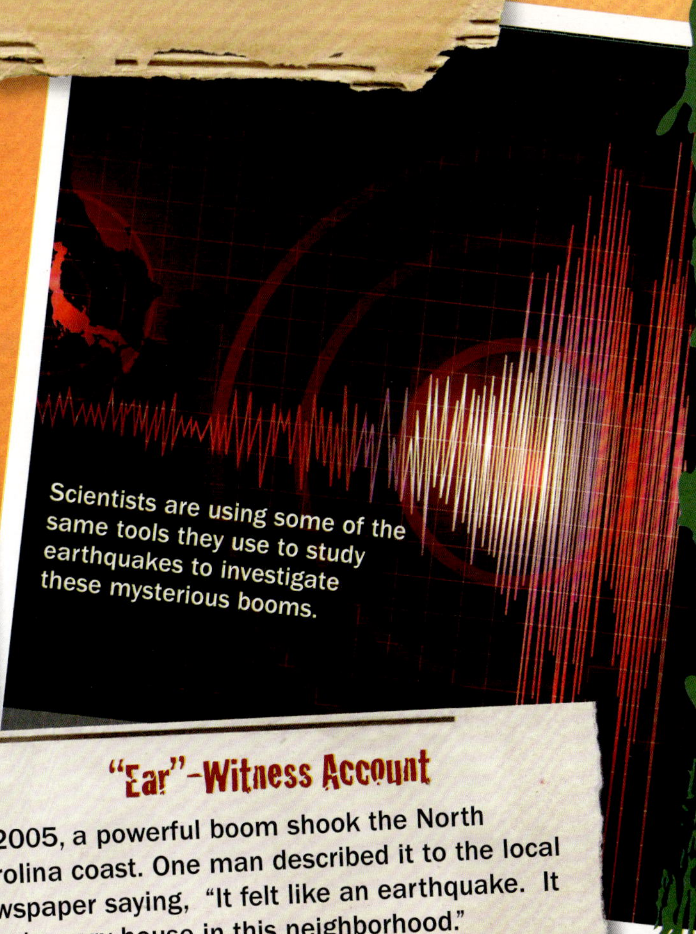

Scientists are using some of the same tools they use to study earthquakes to investigate these mysterious booms.

"Ear"-Witness Account

In 2005, a powerful boom shook the North Carolina coast. One man described it to the local newspaper saying, "It felt like an earthquake. It shook every house in this neighborhood."

Puzzling Patterns

Strange designs cover the land in many parts of the world. Peculiar patterns can be seen in fields. Others show up in desert sands. In Peru, the desert floor is decorated with huge drawings. They show animals, plants, and people. Giant circles in cornfields appear around the world. Tracks in the soil from moving rocks puzzle visitors to California's Racetrack Playa. These strange markings leave more questions than answers. Who made the designs? How were they made? And why?

Mysterious patterns cover land around the world.

"You are a problem
And a rune;
You are mystery,
Writ on a stone."

—Hilda Doolittle, poet

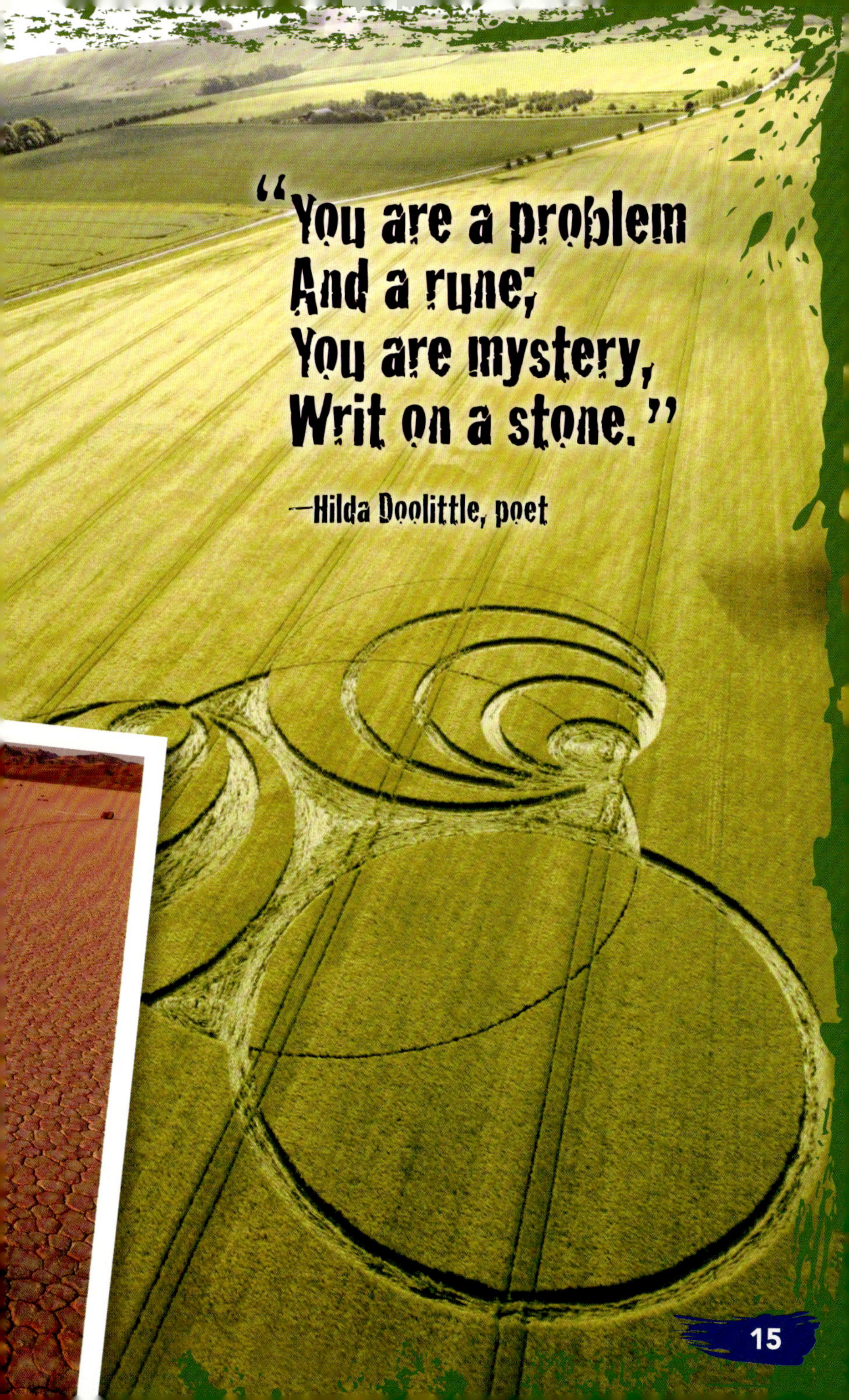

Creepy Crops

Crop circles are designs that appear suddenly in farm fields. Inside large circles, crop stalks are flattened. The bent stalks and the standing stalks form a design. Crop circles can be a few simple circles or detailed patterns. They are best viewed from above.

Many crop circles appeared in England in the 1980s. But they have been seen around the world. Some crop circles have been hoaxes. But some researchers say many of the circles are too perfect to have been made by people.

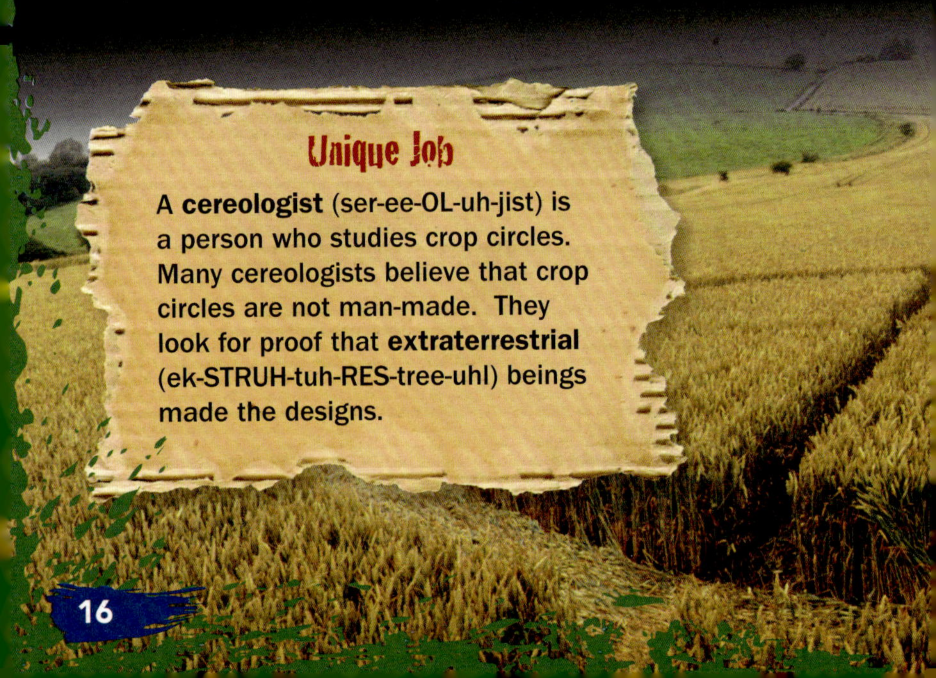

Unique Job

A **cereologist** (ser-ee-OL-uh-jist) is a person who studies crop circles. Many cereologists believe that crop circles are not man-made. They look for proof that **extraterrestrial** (ek-STRUH-tuh-RES-tree-uhl) beings made the designs.

Huge Hoax

In 1991, Doug Bower and Dave Chorley claimed the crop circles in Southern England as their work. They said they began making the designs as a prank in 1978. They continued for nearly 20 years. Still, about 100 new crop circles occur every year in England. Are they all hoaxes?

One Theory

Scientists are looking for a link between crop circles and **vortices** (VAWR-tuh-seez). A vortex is a whirling mass of air that draws things toward its center. Crops on the ground could be gently bent over by these spinning air masses. The landscape of southern England lends itself to the formation of vortices.

DIG DEEPER!

Anatomy of a Crop Circle

What's the big deal? Is a crop circle just a bunch of broken grass? Read more to find out why these circles are so curious.

Crop circles can be beautiful and baffling.

Birds often avoid flying over the crop circle airspace.

The stalks of the grain from a crop circle are often bent to a 90-degree angle without breaking.

Some fields have had multiple crop circles over the years.

Most crop circles are found in England within 20 miles of the mysterious Stonehenge. Like crop circles, no one knows how the stones appeared.

Drawings in the Desert

In the 1920s, pilots flew over Peru for the first time. They reported seeing huge designs on the desert floor. There were hundreds of drawings. They showed animals, plants, and people. The largest pictures are about as long as two football fields. These **geoglyphs** (JEE-o-glifs) make up the Nazca Lines. The Nazca people made them 2,000 years ago. They scraped away the top layer of earth to reveal the dirt below. But one question remains. Why did the ancient people make designs best seen from the sky?

Line Art

The Nazca Lines form a variety of pictures. More than 70 of the designs show animals such as monkeys, llamas, jaguars, hummingbirds, fish, spiders, lizards, sharks, and orcas. Others are simple geometric patterns, trees, flowers, and even people.

The Nazca people fished in the ocean 15 miles away. Heavy rains, flooding, and storms in the ocean may have led to the death of the Nazca people 1,500 years ago.

Religious Rites

Most researchers agree that the lines are related to the Nazca's religious beliefs. Some say the lines are sacred paths leading to places of worship.

Mystery Map

Check out these mysterious locations in our world.

Pennsylvania

The official Ringing Rocks State Park can be found in Pennsylvania. Rocks have also been heard in Mexico, England, Scotland, and Australia.

Missouri

Perhaps 1 in 150 people has observed ball lightning. It was recently seen in Joplin, Missouri in 2011.

North Carolina

Mysterious booms have been heard off the coast of North Carolina as well as in New York State and countries around the world.

Peru

The Nazca lines can be found south of Lima, Peru. The oldest lines date back to 500 BC.

England

Crop circles were first reported in England. Today, they appear to be a worldwide phenomena.

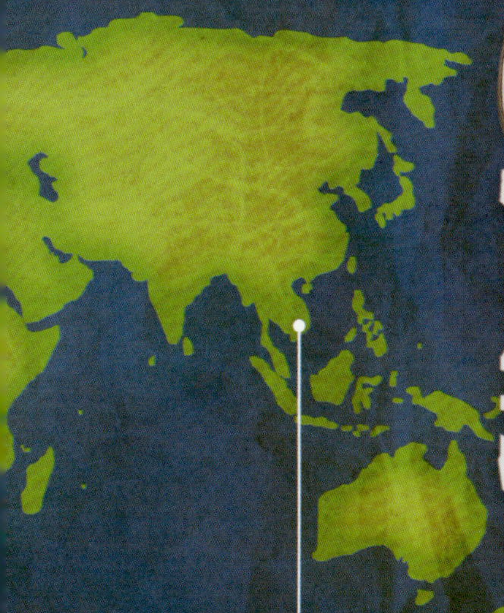

Thailand

This country has celebrated a religious holiday with the Naga fireballs for hundreds of years.

STOP! THINK...

- What places would you like to explore?
- What mysterious event do you think has had the biggest impact on history?
- Why do you think there are no mysterious events shown in Africa?

The Crooked Forest

In a small forest in Poland, 400 strange pine trees grow crookedly. Each tree bends 90 degrees to the north. The mysterious trees were planted in 1930. Hundreds of normal trees grow around them. Those trees grow straight up. Some people believe the bend in the trees was made by people. They think people somehow held the trees down until they grew in a different direction. Scientists have studied the trees' size. The bend must have happened 7 to 10 years after they were planted. It's still not clear why or how someone would do this.

In the ancient art of bonsai (bahn-zahy), trees are planted in small pots and intentionally bent to look old and weathered.

Some people believe the trees in Poland were designed to be used as bent panels in boats.

Racing Rocks

Death Valley is the hottest place in North America. In this desert with the spooky name, mysterious rocks baffle scientists. Within Death Valley is a place called Racetrack Playa. The name comes from the tracks left by rocks. The rocks range in size. Some are just pebbles. But the largest is a 700-pound boulder. Some trails are more than 1,000 feet long. Somehow these rocks move across the flat land. No one has ever seen the racing rocks in motion. But visitors can see the trails they leave behind.

A Fitting Name

Death Valley is located in the Mojave (moh-HAH-vee) Desert of California. The area usually receives less than two inches of rain each year. Death Valley holds the record for the highest temperature in the western hemisphere—134 degrees!

Eyewitness Account

In 2010, a group of students visited the rocks at Racetrack Playa. One student, Andrew Ryan, said, "It's surprising when you see how big some of these boulders are. You think, *How can something that big get blown around?*"

Unexplained Events

The events in this chapter are varied and strange. But they all defy logic. One occurs only in the mind. Another happened more than 100 years ago. The third shocks people every year.

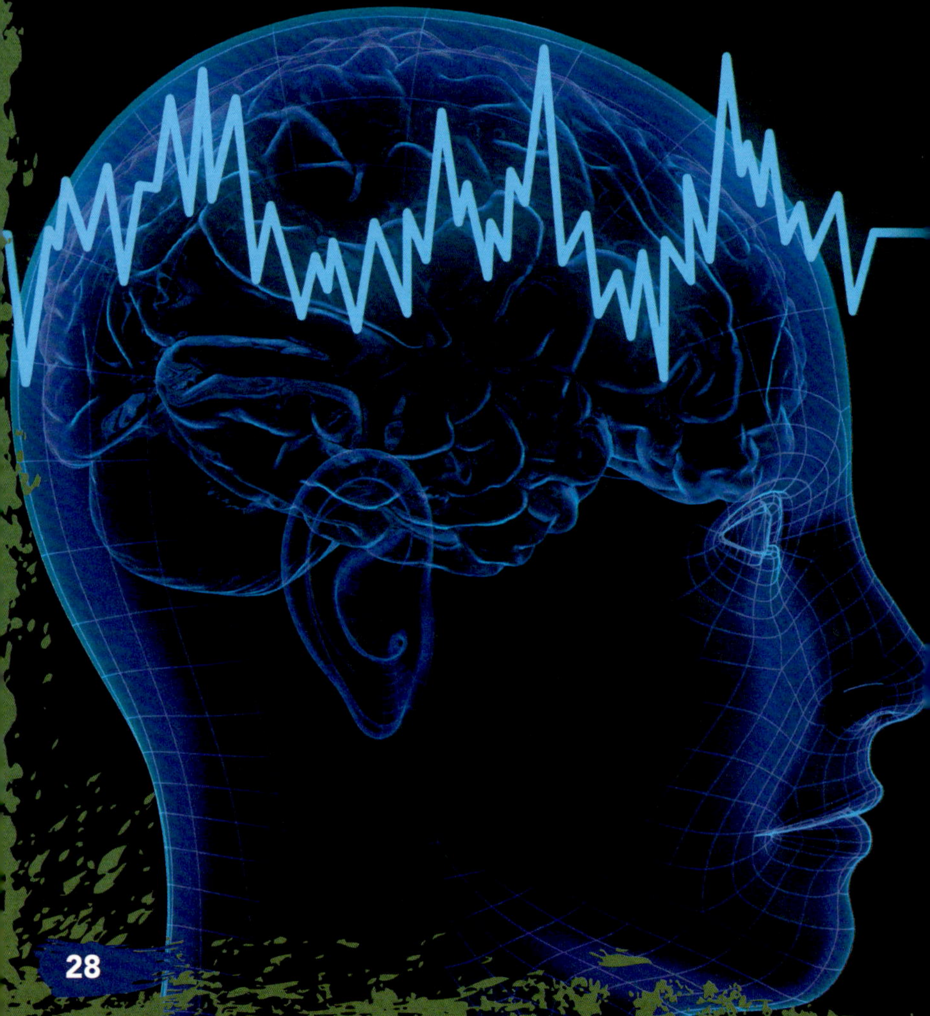

Been There, Done That

Déjà vu (DEY-zhah VOO) is a French term. It means "already seen." It refers to a strange event in the brain. From time to time, people get an odd feeling. They can feel some place is familiar—even if they haven't been there before. They are sure they have seen it before. People often describe the event as *eerie*.

Brain researchers are studying déjà vu. They are just beginning to solve the mystery. They say it might be caused by an overlap of a person's short-term and long-term memories.

The Opposite of Déjà Vu

Jamais vu (ZHA-me VOO) is a French term that means "never seen." It describes a familiar situation that a person does not recognize. A person with *jamais vu* feels that he or she is experiencing something for the first time even though it is a familiar event.

I Knew That!

Have you ever known something without knowing how you knew it? Perhaps you learned it long ago and forgot. Or maybe you were using **extrasensory perception** (**ESP**). It means being able to know things without using normal senses. Usually, we use touch, sight, hearing, taste, or smell to learn about the world. But some people say they are able to predict the future using ESP. Other people say they can use ESP to communicate with close family and friends.

Intuition

ESP may not exist, but intuition does. When people understand something intuitively, they understand it instantly. Scientists believe people who use intuition draw on past information and very small clues to make decisions.

Scientists test the power of ESP by asking people to predict what shape is on a random card.

Scientists test ESP by asking people to predict the future. They want to ask questions that could only be answered using ESP. It is hard to be sure the people are not receiving any hints. Scientists are still unsure if ESP really exists.

DIG DEEPER!

Extra Information

Some people think ESP exists, but most scientists doubt it. It may be that it appears ESP is happening when it's really something simpler. Some people may be really good at reading others' expressions and body language. Others believe that ESP happens when someone is able to feel waves of thought in the air. Still others think that ESP is only a strange coincidence. What do you think?

John Edward

John Edward is best known for his ESP abilities. Ever since he was a child, people believed he had special powers. People who have lost loved ones ask him for help. Over the last 20 years, John Edward has tried to use ESP to connect thousands of people to those who are no longer alive. Many people think his findings are accurate. Other people believe he is correct only 10 to 20 percent of the time.

Close Connection

Have someone you are close to try to guess what you're thinking about. Is your friend able to read your thoughts?

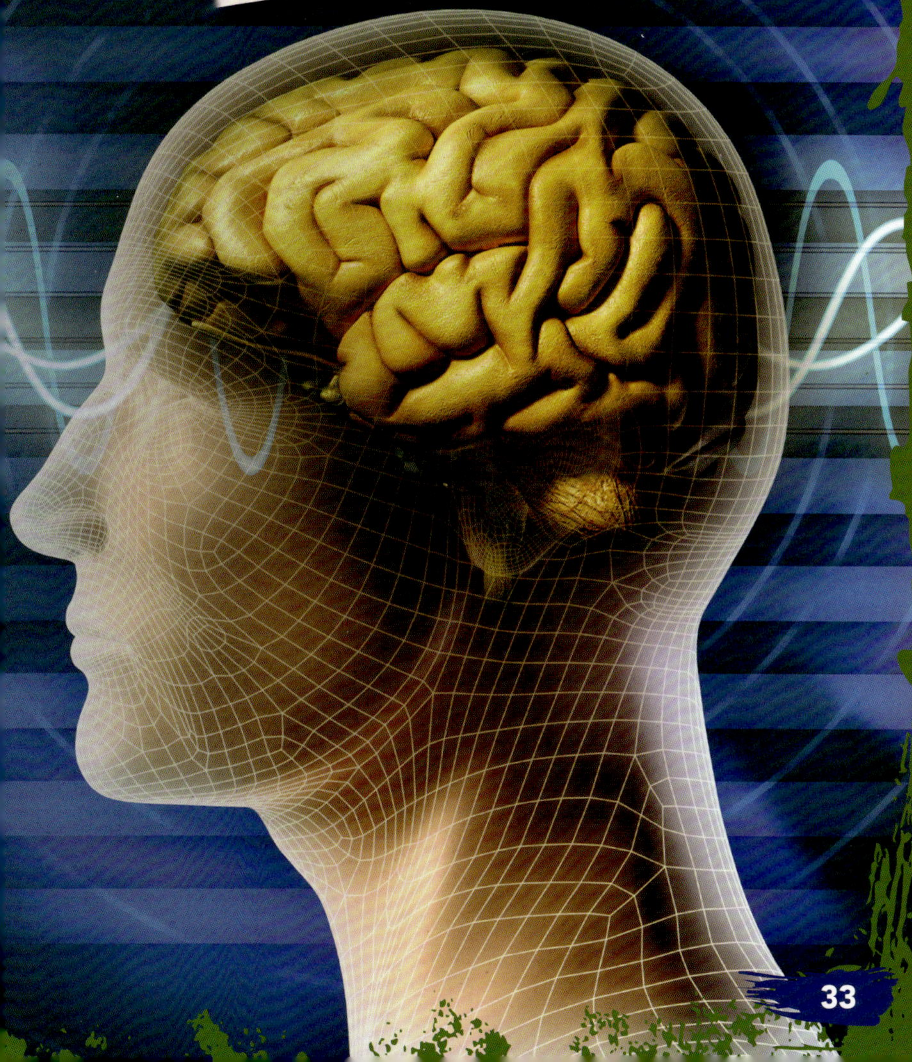

A Powerful Blast

In 1908, a sudden blast shook Siberia, Russia. The explosion flattened 800 square miles of forest. Eighty million trees lay on the ground. All of them were pointing away from the **epicenter**. Forty miles from the center, the blast threw a man from his chair. He said flames filled the sky. He got so hot he thought his shirt was on fire. This explosion became known as the Tunguska Event. It has puzzled scientists for more than a century.

Falling Sky?

An **asteroid** is the most likely cause of the Tunguska Event. The space rock probably exploded over Siberia with the force of 185 **atomic bombs**.

Some people believed the explosion was so strong it must have been caused by a god.

Eyewitness Account

A man was working at a nearby trading post on the day of the Tunguska Event. This is what he described,

> "Suddenly in the north sky…the sky was split in two, and high above the forest the whole northern part of the sky appeared covered with fire….At that moment there was a bang in the sky and a mighty crash…. The crash was followed by a noise like stones falling from the sky, or of guns firing. The earth trembled."

It's Raining *What?*

Imagine walking down the street when frogs begin to fall from the sky like rain. After a few minutes, the shower ends. The ground is covered with frogs. It may sound like fiction, but animal rains are a fact!

People have reported **bizarre** rains for thousands of years. Frogs, fish, worms, and mussels have fallen around the world. Scientists accept the fact that animals rain from the sky. Yet they are unable to explain how this happens.

Rain of Fish

It rains fish every summer in Honduras. To make it even stranger, the fish that fall from the sky are not **native** to the region. Locals mark the event by cooking and eating the fish.

Strange Rains

Check out some of the strangest weather our world has ever seen.

1861
Singapore
fish

1873
Missouri
frogs

1877
South Carolina
baby alligators

1894
England
jellyfish

1901
Minnesota
frogs

1947
Louisiana
fish

1989
Australia
fish

2007
Argentina
spiders

2009
Japan
frogs

2011
Scotland
worms

Tools of the Trade

Scientists are trained to ask questions, form **hypotheses**, and test their theories. This scientific method can be used to answer questions such as "What causes Naga fireballs?" or "Do earthquakes affect the weather?" Scientists use a wide variety of tools to observe mysterious phenomena and test their theories. The work of these researchers helps us discover the truth about our strange world.

A Geiger counter detects energy that may be greater or smaller than normal.

Some things need to be seen to be believed. A camera is an important tool in recording strange events.

Night vision goggles allow researchers to see in the dark.

A seismograph records vibrations in the Earth.

Microphones allow scientists to record odd sounds. Video cameras can capture events while people are at a safe distance.

Investigators should always carry a notebook with them. It's useful for recording observations in the field.

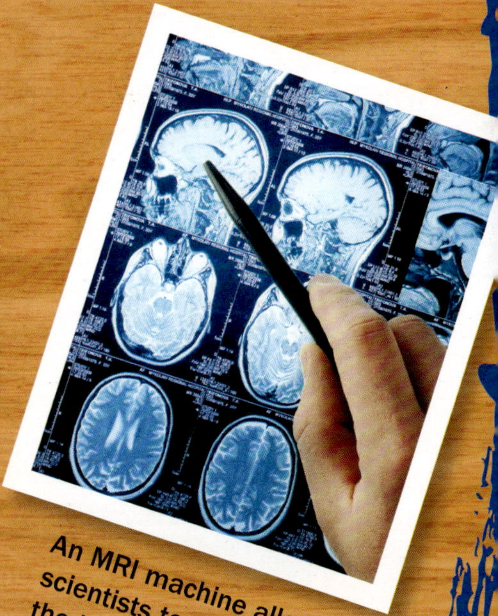

An MRI machine allows scientists to see how the brain works.

The Truth Is Out There

Many years ago, the brightest minds in the world said the Earth was flat. People thought fevers and earthquakes were caused by angry gods. Science has **debunked** those myths. But many mysteries are unexplained even today. Researchers have solid theories about ball lightning and déjà vu. But that is not the case with ringing rocks, crop circles, and animal rains. These events are harder to explain. One thing is certain. Future scientists will have plenty of questions left to answer about this wild world!

What do YOU think caused these events?

Glossary

asteroid—a rock that orbits the sun

atomic bomb—a highly dangerous nuclear weapon

baffled—confused or puzzled

bizarre—strange or unusual

Buddhist—a person who practices the religion of Buddhism

cereologist—a person who studies crop circles, especially those who believe the circles are not man-made

crop circles—large geometric designs created by flattened stalks in fields of grain, best viewed from above

debunked—proven false

déjà vu—a brain event that causes a feeling of having experienced something before

diabase—a type of rock that makes up Earth's crust and is also found in Ringing Rocks State Park in Pennsylvania

epicenter—the exact center or focal point

extrasensory perception (ESP)—the possible ability of some people to know about the environment without using their five senses

extraterrestrial—outside the limits of Earth

geoglyphs—large designs created on the ground

hoaxes—tricks designed to get people to believe something is true when it is not

hypotheses—ideas created to explain some unexplained phenomena

ignite—to set on fire

jamais vu—a brain event that causes a feeling of never having experienced a familiar event before

Naga—dragons that are believed to live in the Mekong River in Thailand

native—living naturally in a place

orbs—spherical objects

phenomena—things that are out of the ordinary and excite people's interest and curiosity

religious—relating to a belief in a higher power

silicon—a nonmetallic element found in Earth's soil

theory—a set of facts or principles analyzed and used to explain a phenomenon

vapor—moisture visible in the air as mist, clouds, fumes, or smoke

vortices—spinning air masses; plural of *vortex*

Index

Bibliography

Allen, Judy. *Unexplained: An Encyclopedia of Curious Phenomena, Strange Superstitions, and Ancient Mysteries.* Kingfisher, 2006.

Read about many of the phenomena discussed in this book, including raining frogs and crop circles. You will also learn about other phenomena that have baffled scientists for years.

Dennis, Jerry. *It's Raining Frogs and Fishes: Four Seasons of Natural Phenomena and Oddities of the Sky.* HarperPerennial, 1993.

This book investigates strange weather and storms that have occurred throughout history. It discusses the phenomena of raining frogs and fishes.

Helstrom, Kraig. *Crop Circles.* Bellwether Media, 2011.

Investigate crop circles around the world in this book. You will learn about different hypotheses on where the designs come from and explore the history of their sightings around the world.

McMullen, David. *Mystery in Peru: The Lines of Nazca.* Contemporary Perspectives, 1997.

This book discusses the mystery of the Nazca Lines in Peru. It makes hypotheses on what they were used for in ancient times by the Incas.

More to Explore

Poland's Crooked Forest

http://news.discovery.com/earth/polands-crooked-forest-mystery-110628.html

Search for "Poland's crooked forest" to learn more about this mystery and see more photographs.

Nazca Lines

http://www.go2peru.com/nazca_lines.htm

Read all about the Nazca Lines on this website. Information and a photo gallery are provided.

Ringing Rocks

http://www.unmuseum.org/ringrock.htm

This article tells about the ringing rocks in Pennsylvania. It even contains a link to recordings of the ringing so you can hear for yourself what the rocks sound like.

National Geographic for Kids

http://kids.nationalgeographic.com/kids/

National Geographic's website for kids provides information on a variety of topics from around the world and provides photos and videos of natural landscapes and wildlife as well as games and other activities.

About the Authors

Lisa Greathouse grew up in Brooklyn, New York, and graduated from the State University of New York with a bachelor's degree in English and journalism. She was a journalist with The Associated Press for 10 years and covered news on everything from science and technology to business and politics. She has also worked as a magazine editor for the food industry, a website editor for a university, and an author of many education publications. She is married with two children and resides in Southern California. She always carries a notebook so she can record mysterious events as they happen.

Stephanie Kuligowski has a bachelor's in journalism degree from the University of Missouri and a master's degree in teaching from National Louis University. She worked as a newspaper reporter and columnist before becoming a teacher. Stephanie taught fifth grade for seven years. She lives with her husband and their two children in Crystal Lake, Illinois, where she loves to practice ESP.